Tough Questions Answered

BY DOUG POWELL

C·C

Tough Questions Answered
By Doug Powell

© 2022 Core Christianity
13230 Evening Creek Drive
Suite 220-222
San Diego, CA 92128

All rights reserved. No part of this book may be reproduced or transmitted in any form or by any means, electronic or mechanical, including photocopying, recording, or by any information storage and retrieval system, without permission in writing from the publisher.

Design and Creative Direction by Metaleap Creative

Printed in the United States of America

First Printing—July 2021

CONTENTS

03   CHAPTER ONE   Science
Doesn't science make religion unnecessary?
Why should I believe something I can't see?
Doesn't science disprove the Bible's account of creation?
Doesn't science disprove miracles?
Doesn't science disprove the resurrection?

13   CHAPTER TWO   World Religions
Why is Christianity so exclusive?
What about Buddhism?
What about Islam?
What about the New Age Movement?
What about people who are spiritual but not religious?
What about atheism?

27   CHAPTER THREE   The Bible
Isn't the Bible just a bunch of myths?
Isn't the Bible a bunch of random stories?
Why are the Old and New Testaments so different?
Are the prophecies in the Bible worth taking seriously
Don't the Gospels contradict each other?
Why should the apostles be trusted?

41   CHAPTER FOUR   Morality
Isn't the Bible's view of sexuality overly restrictive?
Isn't the Bible's view of gender outdated and oppressive?
Doesn't the Bible support slavery?
Doesn't the Bible's view of sin teach you to hate yourself?
Doesn't the Bible's view of judgment teach you to despise non-Christians?
How can God be loving with so much evil in the world?

INTRODUCTION

Every weekday on the radio, I receive calls from people wrestling with tough questions. They long to have confidence in their faith, but they question their salvation, fearing they have done something to jeopardize their standing before God. And they don't know what the Bible says about the difficult circumstances of their lives. This is why Core Christianity exists—to answer your tough questions. We want to help you dig deep into the Scriptures—to see for yourself how the gospel of Jesus Christ has the power to transform your life.

But more and more, I hear of people who listen to Core Radio so they can grow in their own ability to answer tough questions. They want to share their faith with family members, coworkers, and neighbors, but fear they won't have answers to the tough questions they ask. At Core Christianity, we also want to equip you to engage the people around you with the truth of God's word. You don't have to be a pastor or trained theologian to field tough questions; you just need the right tools.

In this booklet, skilled apologist Doug Powell provides those tools. He walks you through some of the most difficult questions about the Bible and the Christian life that you might encounter. His clear and simple answers will help strengthen your faith as you see that the truths proclaimed in the Scriptures and upheld throughout history are true. But more than strengthening your own faith, this resource can also serve as a valuable tool for equipping you and others to engage in conversations about your beliefs. We hope it gives you greater confidence and wisdom as you live out your Christian faith before a watching world, "always being prepared to make a defense to anyone who asks you for a reason for the hope that is in you" (1 Pet. 3:15). —Pastor Adriel

CHAPTER ONE

Science

DOESN'T SCIENCE MAKE RELIGION UNNECESSARY?

One of the most common misunderstandings about religious faith is that it's incompatible with science. The implication is that in a pre-scientific world everything was explained by appealing to God (or gods) because there was no other explanation available. Advances in our understanding of how the world works—scientific knowledge—made appealing to God less and less necessary. And as scientific achievements grow, there is less need for God as an explanation for how the world works. Some go so far to say that belief in God hinders science because it discourages investigation of the world.

At the core of this objection is a confusion of *how* and *why*. They are two different questions that can be asked of the same thing. The answers will be different, but also related—not contradictory. Let's say someone asks you how an airplane flies. You would explain how the shape of the wing forces air to flow faster across the top of the wing than the bottom, which makes the air pressure above the wing decrease, creating lift. That's *how*. But what if someone asks *why* aerodynamics works that way? Explaining Bernoulli's Principle is only another description. It isn't an explanation of why it exists or where it came from. Those aren't things science can answer. Science is a technical description of *how* the world works, not where the principles came from or *why* they work.

Because science describes the world, it relies on observation. Theories are formulated to describe the observations, and then experiments are done to confirm or disprove the theories. In order for this system to work, the forces at work in the world must be uniform so that the same thing will happen under the same conditions every time. The apple always falls from the tree, thanks to the force of gravity. But no matter how many times scientists observe the apple fall from the tree, it never reveals where gravity came from.

In an atheistic scientific worldview, the universe spontaneously came into being by random chance. And by chance, part of what sprang into existence were laws of nature that control all the physical things that suddenly existed. By chance, these laws organized the universe in such a way that at least one of the chance planets formed an atmosphere conducive to life. By chance, non-living matter spontaneously became alive, which—by chance, over long periods of time—developed into human beings with the self-awareness and intelligence to observe the universe. Given that science requires order and uniformity to make sense of its observations, does it really make sense to appeal to random chance as the explanation for the *why* of the order we see? In this view of the world, who's to say the laws couldn't randomly change? If that's how the universe came into existence, couldn't it cease to exist in the same way? If random chance is the basis for the existence of the universe, then no one should ever jump on a trampoline since the law of gravity may spontaneously change in mid-air, stranding you or sending you into space.

A better explanation for the order in the universe that we observe and rely on for day-to-day life is that it was designed, and therefore it has a designer. A better explanation for the beginning of the universe is that there is a transcendent being who began it. And because there is intention in both the existence and order of the universe, there is meaning in it. There is a *why*. Religion seeks to answer the specifics about the *why* question, not the *how*. Science answers the *how*. And if both are properly understood, then the answers complement, not contradict each other. Not only that, but if God is the *why*, then God is what makes scientific inquiry possible in the first place. That means the existence of science makes God necessary, not unnecessary.

WHY SHOULD I BELIEVE SOMETHING I CAN'T SEE?

Our five senses tell us many things about the world. You can close your eyes, pinch your nose, or plug your ears, but in general they are always collecting data. We rely on our senses so much that sometimes we think of them as our best source of knowledge. And because science is based on observation, it's a way of precisely articulating what our senses detect. With all the marvelous advantages science has given the world, sometimes people make the mistake of *scientism*, which is thinking scientific knowledge is the best—or even the only—kind of knowledge there is.

But there are many ways we know things that don't have anything to do with science. For example, take the phrase *Science is the best kind of knowledge*. What scientific observation did that come from? None, of course. It's a philosophical statement. And if a person tried to make a case for it, they'd have to reason by using philosophical arguments, not scientific experiments. Reasoning, therefore, is a way of knowing things. Intuition (such as knowing there is such a thing as right and wrong) is another.

The fact is, we all believe things that our senses cannot detect. Have you ever actually *seen* gravity? No, only the effect it has on objects. Have you ever seen a number? No, only its symbol. How about the laws of logic? Just try to say something that makes sense without intuitively using them! How about love or justice or time? Believe in those? We all do.

Sometimes we rely on authorities for our beliefs. Has a doctor ever diagnosed you with strep throat? If so, did you believe them? Do you believe George Washington or Julius Caesar ever existed? The documentary evidence for them leaves little doubt. You may not have read all the material, but there are many historians who have, and we trust their authority.

Imagine you're on the jury of a murder trial. You're being asked to believe in an action you didn't see, and to examine the effects of that action to determine its cause. You'll probably be presented with scientific evidence. Unless you are a forensic scientist yourself, you'll have to trust the authority of the expert witness to understand it. But that's not all to the case. The lawyers will present reasons and use logic to guide you to the truth (hopefully!). And the reason you're on the jury is because the action—murder—is wrong, and you are part of the process of seeking justice. Science, reasoning, moral intuition, and reliance on authorities all intersect, contributing different ways of knowing the truth. And that should be the goal of all belief: truth.

When it comes to God—an immaterial, transcendent being—the reason to believe is much the same as believing in anything else. Does believing in God explain what we see in the world? Does it make sense of my experience? Does a theistic worldview create contradictions or incoherencies? This last question depends on which God is in view, of course, but that's a different question.

In the case of the God of the Bible, God is the maker of all things outside of himself. He's not only the maker of everything that can be known, but all the ways by which we can know them. Logic, the uniformity of the universe, morality—all the intellectual tools we use to evaluate and judge claims must come from God. And that means that without God, you can't justify how you know anything at all. Therefore, although we can't see God, we're justified in believing in him by necessity.

DOESN'T SCIENCE DISPROVE THE BIBLE'S ACCOUNT OF CREATION?

Although the Bible tells us everything we need to know about God, our need of salvation, and how to practice faith, it's not an exhaustive encyclopedia of knowledge. And although it applies to all people throughout history in all parts of the world, we have to remind ourselves that the Bible is a pre-scientific book written for pre-scientific people to understand. The discipline of science was not a category its authors or original audiences used to understand the text. Sometimes it's hard to keep that in mind as we read Scripture. But to treat the Bible as a scientific text would be like using the background of the Mona Lisa to navigate the river in the picture.

When the Bible talks about the origin of the universe and the beginnings of Earth, it describes the process in a sequence ordered into days: light, atmosphere, dry ground and vegetation, stars, fish and birds, land animals and human beings. There have been many ways of trying to understand the description of creation. Some scholars recognize poetry, where the second three days populate the first three days (stars in light, fish and birds in sea and air, land animals and humans on land). Some see it as an attack on the polytheistic demigods of the pagan cultures surrounding the Israelites, showing how one true God made all things by his word.

But some scholars have tried to understand the text in scientific terms. As a sequence, it broadly follows what we know about planet formation and how the world developed, and so it's tempting to view it through a scientific lens. However, there is no description of *how* God did his work other than by speaking. Even without the debate over the length of the days of creation, there is not much data for science to work with before speculation hijacks the text. If the Bible really is God's revelation about himself, he either did a poor job explaining how he created everything or that wasn't the point in the first place.

There is one thing every interpretation of the text agrees on: God created everything. How he did it doesn't seem to be the focus. Despite the vast body of scientific knowledge that has been acquired since Moses recorded Genesis, there's no sufficient explanation for how the universe came into being, how everything came from nothing.

As a result, Science and the Bible are answering different questions. Science answers process: *how* the world works. The Bible answers agency: *who* made it in the first place. They don't contradict each other because they aren't asking the same question. In fact, science complements the creation account by providing details not in Scripture. The door to conflict opens only when science is taken as the main emphasis of the creation story.

DOESN'T SCIENCE DISPROVE MIRACLES?

God is always at work in the world. The vast majority of the time, he sustains it through forces that are so consistent and reliable that science describes them as the laws of nature. Whether this is a direct work or whether God created these forces as a secondary means is debated by theologians. Either way, they're part of God's providence—his normal way of interacting with creation.

In fact, God's normal action is so consistent that the regularity of the universe provides the fundamental starting point for science. It is that regularity that is studied and tested, and it is what makes predicting what will happen under certain conditions possible.

A miracle is when God acts in an unusual way. Miracles bring God glory and act as evidence he can be trusted. Prophets were given miracles to verify that they spoke for God. Jesus and the apostles performed miracles as a way of proving their authority. And the miracles always did good, reflecting the character of God, their source. Miracles aren't a violation of the laws of nature, but sometimes they do suspend them. Because the source of the miracles is God, and he is also the source of the regularity of the universe, then his unusual action isn't a violation of the laws of nature. Both are actions of the same person.

Miracles—by necessity—are rare because they're events that are dramatically contrasted against the regularity of the universe. If miracles were repeated events, then they would be studied as events that happen under the right circumstances. And if miracles were frequent, they would lose their impact, and therefore their usefulness as a tool of communication.

Because science is the discipline of describing the workings of the regularity seen in creation, miracles are beyond the scope of what it can explain. Some miraculous claims can be explained through science, but all that proves is that the alleged miracle was false, not that miracles aren't possible. And scientific advances have made things that once sounded miraculous possible, such as air travel or talking to someone on the other side of the world in real time. But biblical miracles—the resurrection, the parting of the Red Sea, the virgin birth, the feeding of the 5,000, turning water to wine—are not those kinds of things.

Some philosophers have rejected miracles because we judge what we haven't seen by what we have. And when we hear of something wildly unusual happening, we're skeptical of it because the normal way of the world is more probable. When we're confronted with something counter to our experience and the experience of most other people, then we should reject it. On the face of it, this seems like common sense. And yet consider this: How many people do you personally know who have won millions in a lottery, found a buried treasure, been struck by lightning, or been elected president? The wild improbability of any of those things happening can't be proof against them because they *do* happen, of course.

Instead of proving miracles can't happen, science helps us to better recognize miracles. By drawing the boundaries of the normal workings of creation, science creates a way to recognize events outside of the frame—miracles.

DOESN'T SCIENCE DISPROVE THE RESURRECTION?

The scientific method involves observing something in the world, theorizing an explanation for it, testing that theory, making additional observations, and doing more testing. The cycle continues until a reasonably reliable explanation can be made. Making repeated observations and conducting tests other scientists can repeat is fundamental to scientific inquiry. It's also what makes it difficult or even impossible as a way of studying historical events—things that happen only once and cannot be repeated. In those cases—such as the origin of the universe—the effects of the event are studied and inferences are made to explain the cause.

The claim that Jesus was resurrected from the dead is a historical event that can't be observed, tested, or repeated. Medical science does have overwhelming evidence that the dead don't resurrect to life. The exception of near death experiences may provide some evidence for the potential of a conscious state persisting for a time after a person is declared medically dead, but given that the people who have experienced this have been resuscitated within minutes or hours—not resurrected three days later—they aren't very helpful. Also, people who have had near death experiences do eventually die again, unlike the resurrection of Jesus.

Ironically, in an atheistic scientific worldview, the resurrection of Jesus actually is a possibility. If, by random chance, the universe sprang into existence from nothing, and if, by random chance, life came to existence through non-life, then why should the resurrection be seen as impossible? Couldn't Jesus resurrect from the dead through random chance? Isn't it an example of life coming from non-life? In an atheistic scientific worldview, the cause wouldn't be an act of God, but it would still be a resurrection. Therefore, science doesn't disprove the resurrection.

The best evidence for the resurrection is found in the historical effects following it. Jesus' disciples believed they encountered him after his death. According to tradition, eleven of the twelve were martyred for proclaiming the resurrection. Saul of Tarsus, a Pharisee who persecuted Christians for heresy, believed he encountered the resurrected Jesus and radically reoriented his life because of it. He became known as Paul and spent the next 30 years or so traveling throughout the Roman Empire, spreading Jesus' teachings. According to tradition, he was martyred for proclaiming the truth of the resurrection. Then there's Jesus' brother James. John 7:5 says Jesus' brothers didn't believe in him during his earthly ministry. Mark 3:21 says Jesus' family thought he was out of his mind. And yet James believed he encountered Jesus after his death. He even went on to be the leader of the church in Jerusalem. In fact, he was so convinced Jesus was God incarnate that he was martyred, according to tradition. What kind of evidence would convince *you* that your own brother was God incarnate?

CHAPTER TWO

World Religions

WHY IS CHRISTIANITY SO EXCLUSIVE?

Religious faith is not an opinion, like having a favorite band or restaurant. It's a set of beliefs about the nature of reality. Comparing different religions can be difficult because they often use different terms or have different definitions for things. But there are certain core ideas addressed by every religion—every worldview, for that matter. Who is God? What is the world? What is humankind? What is our problem? What is the solution?

Every religion and worldview answers those questions differently, and each of them claim to be true. That means either all religions are false, or only one of them is true.

Sometimes Christianity is criticized for being exclusive, as if Christians are somehow culturally bigoted or unfairly dismissive of alternative views or other cultures. But the truth is that all religions are exclusive. That's the very definition of truth: it accurately describes reality, and as such excludes all other explanations.

Think about Christianity's answers to the five questions:

Who is God? God is a personal, transcendent, infinite, unchanging, self-existent, perfect being who created all things, wants to be known, and therefore reveals himself.

What is the world? The world is everything that exists apart from God.

It was created by him, and he interacts with it, yet is not a part of it.

What is humankind? People are a special creation of God, bearing his image and given the responsibility of being stewards of his creation during their one life on Earth.

What is the problem? People are separated from God by sin, a failure to keep God's law.

What is the solution? Reconciliation with God comes through the work of Jesus Christ on the cross. He took the punishment for the sins of all who believe, and his perfect obedience to God's law is credited to them.

Which answer could be changed and still leave a biblically consistent faith? None of them. These are essential beliefs that make Christianity unique. And if it's true, then it's also exclusive.

In fact, given these essential beliefs, Christianity can't possibly be true *unless* it's exclusive. If any other religion were equally true, then Jesus is not the only way for salvation. And if there is another path to salvation, then Jesus' death becomes a savage, unnecessary torture. That creates a picture of a cruel, uncaring God who is not worthy of worship.

Ironically, when someone complains about the exclusivity of Christianity because they believe all religions are equally valid, they themselves are excluding it, committing the very wrong they condemn. It also reveals a lack of knowledge about other religions, since all of them are equally exclusive.

WHAT ABOUT BUDDHISM?

Buddhism is based on the teachings of Siddhartha Gautama who lived in India about 500 years before Jesus. Although born a prince, he renounced his wealth and position to seek spiritual fulfillment. After finding few satisfying answers in Hinduism, he turned inward and began to focus on meditation. During one of his meditations, he attained enlightenment—the understanding of the nature and meaning of life. As a result, he became known as the Buddha, which means *the enlightened one*. His teachings were passed down through oral tradition until they were written down in the first century BC, and are known as the Tripitaka.

Although there are two main schools of thought and much variation within Buddhism, the five worldview questions help us see the core of the system.

Who is God? Buddhism is an atheistic religion. Most Buddhists believe there is no God or that God is irrelevant. Some Buddhists do pray to a deity, but it is a kind of demigod, not a transcendent, personal, self-existent being who created the universe.

What is the world? The universe was not created, but rather evolved from *dharma*, the law governing reality. It's made of natural laws, teachings of the Buddha, the law of karma, ideas, and ethics.

What is humankind? People are not distinct from the universe, nor are they individual. Personhood and individuality is an illusion because everything is part of ultimate reality.

What is the problem? The illusion of the individual self creates desire, and desire results in suffering. Because there is no God in Buddhism, there is no God to sin against, and therefore no need for atonement.

Instead, salvation is found in ridding yourself of desire. The Buddha expressed the problem in what he called the Four Noble Truths: (1) suffering exists, (2) suffering is caused by desire, (3) ridding yourself of desire will rid suffering, (4) desire is purged by following the Eightfold Path.

What is the solution? The Eightfold Path: (1) Right knowledge (believing the Four Noble Truths and the Eightfold Path); (2) Right attitude (reject earthly pleasure); (3) Right speech (don't lie or use idle words); (4) Right action (don't kill or steal); (5) Right living (earn a living without harming anything or anyone); (6) Right effort (develop goodness, reject evil); (7) Right mindfulness (be strong and thoughtful, without desire); (8) Right meditation (develop the concentration to meditate). Following the Eightfold Path perfectly leads to nirvana, which is essentially the annihilation of the self and absorption into the impersonal universe. At the end of your life, if you haven't followed the path perfectly, you are reincarnated based on the works of your previous life. This cycle of birth and rebirth repeats until you attain nirvana.

In contrast with Christianity, Buddhism is a system which teaches that you can save yourself. There's no grace, no forgiveness, no love. And without the existence of a personal God, it's hard to see how an impersonal universe could require you to obey laws intended to guide people and judge their choices, such as moral laws. How does an impersonal universe determine if you have kept the law perfectly? How can its judgment be trusted? In Christianity, human beings are special, created in God's image, not illusions to be denied. And they are created with desires and the moral responsibility to desire good things. As a result, Buddhism is not simply a different flavor of religion that is equal to Christianity. The two beliefs are radically different.

WHAT ABOUT ISLAM?

Islam is based on the teaching of Muhammad, who lived in Saudi Arabia about 600 years after Jesus. Muhammad led trade caravans around the region, becoming exposed to many different teachings, including Judaism and Christianity. After marrying the wealthy woman who owned the caravans, he would spend time in prayer and fasting on a mountain near his home in Mecca. During one of these retreats, an angel appeared to Muhammad and told him he was a prophet of Allah (the Arabic word for *God*). Soon after, Muhammad began receiving and sharing messages. As his followers grew, the messages were written down. By the end of his life twenty-two years later, his teaching had united the pagan tribes of Arabia in a common faith for the first time. His messages were collected and became known as the Qur'an (*recitations*), the primary authority for the faith. The faith he preached became known as Islam (*submit*), and its followers Muslims (*submitters*).

In many ways, Islam's view of God is very close to the God of the Bible. In fact, Islam acknowledges much of the Bible as Scripture, and reveres the same prophets—including Jesus (though they reject him as Messiah). But Islam also considers the Bible to be so corrupted that the original text has been almost entirely lost and cannot be trusted. That's why Muhammad—the last prophet—was given the final revelation of the Qur'an.

Who is God? Allah is a transcendent, personal, self-existent being who created all things, and reveals himself.

What is the world? The world is everything that exists apart from God. It was created by him, and he is sovereign over it.

What is humankind? People are God's greatest creation. Their purpose is to obey God rather than know him.

What is our problem? Arrogance and pride keep people from submitting to Allah. There is no sinful nature (as in Christianity), there are only individual sins.

What is the solution? Salvation is through good works, primarily achieved through the Five Pillars: (1) Shahadah—the public proclamation that there is no god but Allah, and Muhammad is his prophet; (2) Salat—the five daily prayers; (3) Zakat—giving 2.5 percent to charity; (4) Seyaam—fasting during the month of Ramadan; (5) Hajj—a pilgrimage to Mecca, done at least once unless it can't be afforded. Unlike Christianity, salvation is based on works, not grace. The Qur'an speaks of good works in terms of a scale, and if they outweigh the bad works, then you will find favor with Allah.

Although the concept of God is very similar to Christianity, Islam rejects the Trinity as a form of polytheism. In Islam, Allah is one person in one substance. This may not seem like an important distinction, but it reveals an internal incoherence in Islamic theology, a fatal flaw. Islam teaches Allah does not change and is self-existent. It also teaches Allah is love. Who does Allah love? Those who obey him, or in a general sense, the world. But the world did not always exist. So who did Allah love before he created the world? It can't be himself since he's only one person and love is a relational attribute. Without someone or something to love, Allah would only be *potentially* loving. To actually become love requires something outside of himself, and that means to be loving means Allah cannot be self-existent. It also means that by creating something to love Allah changes from *potential* love to *actual* love. But Allah cannot change. The theology contradicts itself in at least two places.

Now ask the same question of the Christian concept of God, who is also unchanging, self-existent, and love. Who did God love before creation? Himself, which is made possible because of his trinitarian nature. Each member of the Trinity loves the others. By creating the world, God does not change or need anything outside of himself to be who he is.

The God of the Bible and the god of the Qu'ran are not the same. The biblical God does not have the same philosophical and historical contradictions that Allah has. Islam, therefore, is not compatible with Christianity. Both God and Allah cannot exist.

WHAT ABOUT THE NEW AGE MOVEMENT?

When we look at different religions, we usually want to know who founded them and what their scriptures are. But New Age religions aren't like that. There is no single founder or one authoritative writing. Instead, there is such a wide variety of groups and beliefs that it can be hard to define what it means to be New Age. And yet there are three core teachings they all share, which is what enables us to consider them as a group or a movement: monism, reincarnation, and karma. Although they have no scripture, they borrow these three teachings from the Vedas, the scripture of Hinduism. Because this understanding comes at the beginning of a new astrological age, it is referred to as New Age.

Monism is the belief that reality consists of one single thing. Everything is part of that one thing. There are two schools of thought in monism. Some New Age groups teach there are no actual parts at all. There is no such thing as individuality, and distinctions between things don't actually exist. But most New Age teachings hold that reality is made of parts that come from a single divine energy. God is the impersonal force holding all things together and is in all things. This is called pantheism.

The goal of New Age belief is to reach enlightenment, which is the realization that human beings—by virtue of being a part of reality—are divine. Enlightenment is so difficult to attain that it requires many lifetimes. Therefore there must be reincarnation.

During each lifetime people make advances toward enlightenment, but also can regress by doing bad things. The system that determines the state into which people are reincarnated is called karma.

When we apply the worldview grid to New Age Movements, it looks like this:

Who is God? God is a divine energy enabling and inhabiting everything that exists, and is therefore impersonal and non-transcendent.

What is the world? The world is the reality enabled and inhabited by the divine energy.

What is humankind? People are the product of the divine energy in all things.

What is our problem? People do not realize they are divine.

What is the solution? The purpose of life is personal transformation and healing through self-knowledge. To achieve transformation, two practices are common: crystals and spirit channeling. Crystals are considered to have healing powers and can be used to program the seven centers of energy in the human body called chakras (another idea borrowed from Hinduism). Crystals influence the chakras to lead people to a healthier mindset. There are also energy vortexes in the geological structure of the Earth such as Sedona, Arizona and Asheville, North Carolina. Many New Age practitioners pilgrimage to these places to meditate.

Spirit channelling is the practice of offering yourself as a vehicle to an enlightened spirit so that they can speak through you and offer wisdom to guide people through transformations.

At their core, New Age Movements are works-based religions that offer self-salvation through special knowledge. There is no grace, no forgiveness, no sin, and therefore no need for atonement. Many New Age Movements claim to have a place for Jesus as a good moral teacher, but not as a savior. It sounds accepting and inclusive, but in order to claim Jesus, New Age Movements must redefine him so that he is unrecognizable from the person in the New Testament. In other words, they don't accept him at all.

WHAT ABOUT PEOPLE WHO ARE SPIRITUAL BUT NOT RELIGIOUS?

It's common these days to hear people describe themselves as spiritual but not religious. Obviously, such a vague statement means different things to different people, but in general it's a rejection of what they call organized religion. They see all religions as nothing more than human institutions, and they see Scripture, doctrine, and ceremonies as ways those institutions use their power. Spiritual people acknowledge an innate impulse to believe in God, but don't discriminate between how that faith is expressed. Many spiritual people don't condemn believing in an organized religion, but say that particular way is not for them. The important thing for them is faith itself, not the object or focus of that faith. Their faith is in faith.

This universalism where all beliefs are equally valid sounds tolerant and non-judgmental in a pluralistic society like ours, but it can only be that way by defining faith a certain way. In our culture, faith is usually seen as a kind of wishing, hoping, or even superstition. We hear people say, "*You just have to have faith,*" as if faith is a kind of magic ingredient that makes your wish come true. This reduces faith to mere preference and makes all faith equal.

But biblical faith isn't that kind of thing. In the New Testament, the Greek word for *faith* is *pistis*. *Pistis* means a firm persuasion or conviction. What does it take to be persuaded? Reasons. And what does it take to be convicted? Evidence. Biblical faith is not an opinion, wish, or mere hope, but a belief that can be defended, explained, and investigated.

Think of it this way: Let's say you have five identical bags in front of you, and you get to pick one to keep. How would you choose between them? By looking inside to see which one contains the most valuable thing. If one has a lump of coal, another contains a twig, the third a broken comb, the fourth a paper clip, and the fifth has a gold bar, which one would you pick? Obviously, the gold bar. Why? Because it has the most value. The bag is only as valuable as what it contains. Faith is like the bag. It's only as valuable as its object.

Putting this view through the five worldview questions is meaningless because the first four questions can be answered in any way someone wants. Who is God? Whoever you want him to be. What is the world? Whatever you want it to be, etc. The only question that can really be answered is the last one. What is the solution? The answer is faith. Faith in what? Whatever you want.

The Bible shows that God not only revealed himself as worthy of worship, but he also reveals *how* he should be worshipped. There are a number of examples of people in the Bible whose worship was not accepted by God because it was not done in the way he prescribed. Their faith was in their faith, not in God, and therefore was rejected.

WHAT ABOUT ATHEISM?

Some people describe themselves as neither spiritual nor religious. Sometimes that means they don't believe God exists at all. Others think if God does exist then we can't know anything about him and therefore he's irrelevant. There are also people who describe themselves as agnostic, meaning they don't know if God exists because there's just not enough evidence to decide. All are forms of atheism, the belief that God does not exist or is unnecessary for explaining the way the world is.

Because atheism is not an organized, monolithic belief, there is no system or set of doctrines to apply the five worldview questions to. Yet applying the denial of God to the answers is quite revealing.

Who is God? God does not exist or is irrelevant and unnecessary.

What is the world? The world is a product of random chance.

What is humankind? People are the product of a random chance combination of chemicals in the world.

What is our problem? Some say the problem is religious belief, which is no more than superstition that creates division and is responsible for countless wars and abuse of power. Some believe human beings are inherently good, but lack knowledge. Some believe government and civilization are the problem, while others believe lack of government is the problem.

What is the solution? Depends on the problem of course, but all solutions are grounded in human ability and essential human goodness.

Interestingly, despite the variety of answers to the last two questions, it's the attempt to answer them at all that is the fatal flaw for atheism.

Asking what the problem is assumes something is wrong with the world. But what is meant by *wrong*? And how can the solution be *better*? What is the standard for judging if something is right or wrong, good or bad, better or worse? Those are moral terms that don't merely describe how things are, but also how they should be. If the world and people are nothing more than products of random chance, then where do these laws come from? Atheists often try to account for morality by saying it's the principle of doing more good than harm, and that makes the world better. But that doesn't answer the question of where the moral law came from. Saying something does more good than bad requires the ability to recognize good and bad in the first place. We don't derive the ideas of good and bad from observing the world, we observe the world with the innate ideas of good and bad. The question is how that can be possible. And even if we do recognize something as wrong or bad, *why* should we try to make it better? How can our free actions be judged by a random, chance, impersonal world? They can't, of course.

The moral laws all people intuitively recognize prescribe how we *should* live. That means we can think about our actions before we take them. What kind of things think about actions before taking them? Persons. And could the moral laws be arbitrary or be anything other than what they are? There might be debate over the facts of a situation, but the moral laws we apply to the facts don't and cannot change. There is never a time where torture and murder of babies is okay, for example. The moral law applies to all people at all times. And there can't be a time when the law didn't exist. Therefore the source of the law is a transcendent, unchanging, person. That is a classic description of God. God is, ironically, necessary for atheism to exist.

CHAPTER THREE

The Bible

ISN'T THE BIBLE JUST A BUNCH OF MYTHS?

What would you think if a stranger came up to you and told you God spoke to them? You'd probably ask (politely, of course!) how they knew it was God. What if the stranger replied that God spoke to him from a bush that was on fire, but didn't burn up? You probably wouldn't put much stock in what he said. And what if the stranger told you he wasn't the only one, and that there's an exclusive club of people who all believed God spoke to them as well, but gave each different miracles? One walked on water, another was in the belly of a fish for three days, several predicted events that came true, and one sounds like he caught a ride to heaven in an Uber made of fire. You'd probably think the members of this exclusive club were delusional, untrustworthy historians. To skeptics, this is often how Christianity sounds when we say the Bible is true.

Although the Bible isn't a history book, it does claim to record history. But because it documents a small people group in a part of the world that was insignificant to the world powers of that time, there aren't a lot of records to consult for corroboration. So how do we know any of these things really happened and aren't just myths?

Admittedly, many biblical events, such as the parting of the Red Sea or how the walls of Jericho fell, don't have any evidence except the testimony of Scripture. But the advent of archaeology provides a way of recovering evidence that can corroborate at least some parts of the stories. There have been many claims in the Bible that were dismissed by scholars because the Bible was the only document of record. For example, until recently, some scholars doubted the existence of a historical King David. And the books of Luke and Acts are full of specific names, places, and offices that were thought to prove its *inaccuracy* because there was no other evidence for those things. But in the early '90's an inscription was discovered in northern Israel mentioning the "house of David," proving his historicity. And over the last 150 years, so many inscriptions have been discovered that cite the same rulers and offices recorded by Luke that Luke's Gospel and Acts are now considered trustworthy sources even by non-Christian archaeologists. Several excavations at Jericho have revealed evidence for when the walls fell, and the direction they fell (outward), though *how* it happened can't be known from the ruins.

There's a wealth of evidence for biblical history developed by archaeology, and yet—at best—it's fragmentary. It's like finding stray puzzle pieces—they fit the picture, but leave more holes than they fill. Nevertheless, archaeology does provide reasons for trusting the historical accounts.

Another way we can trust the historicity of the Bible is based on the historical evidence for the resurrection. There are many facts in the Bible about Jesus' death and what happened to him three days later. However, many skeptical scholars think at least some of those are legendary, added to the story later. And yet, there are at least six facts that even the most skeptical biblical scholars accept: (1) Jesus was crucified, (2) Jesus died, (3) Jesus was buried, (4) the tomb was found empty, (5) many friends of Jesus believed they encountered him after his death, (6) some enemies (such as Saul/Paul and Jesus' own brother James) believed they encountered him after his death. These facts are important because these skeptical scholars try to explain what happened to Jesus in different ways: the body was stolen; the disciples went to the wrong tomb; they hallucinated appearances of Jesus; or they made up a legend. But none of those stories make sense of all six facts. For example, what made James believe his own brother was God incarnate so strongly that he was martyred for it? A hallucination? No way. The only story that makes sense of all of the facts is the biblical account. The stories that deny it are the myths.

So what does this have to do with all the other claims of Scripture? The resurrection proves Jesus is who he said he was and that anything he said could be trusted. And part of what he taught was that the Hebrew Bible (the Old Testament) was Scripture. He spoke of Jonah as a historical figure who spent three days in the belly of a giant fish. He didn't treat it as a fish story! He also spoke of Adam and Eve, Noah, the Flood, and the ark as historical. In light of the historical evidence for the resurrection, his authority is enough to justify believing the Bible is historical, not mythical.

ISN'T THE BIBLE A BUNCH OF RANDOM STORIES?

Hansel and Gretel. Snow White. Rapunzel. Sleeping Beauty. What do these stories have to do with each other? Besides being folk tales collected by the Brothers Grimm, nothing. Some people see the Bible the same way. It was written over a span of 1,400 years in three different languages by about forty different people of different social stations ranging from kings to fishermen. And unlike the Brothers Grimm, what they wrote isn't in the same genre; it's all over the map. There's poetry, history, predictions of the future, advice for living wisely, and song lyrics. There are also stories like Adam and Eve; Noah's Ark; Samson; David and Goliath; Jonah and the big fish; Daniel in the lion's den; Shadrach, Meshach, and Abednego; and Jesus turning water into wine. On the surface, there doesn't seem to be much tying the stories and other material together. And too often, these stories have been treated as merely morality tales for children, as if *that* is their common thread.

To understand how the books and stories are united, imagine you have three flashlights, each with a different colored filter—red, green, and blue. If you shine the red light on a picture, you can see the image, but it is tinted red. Many details and nuances of the image aren't revealed in purely red light. Now do the same thing with the other two. Each flashlight tints the image a certain way, revealing some features, but not others. But what happens if you point all three colors at the image at the same time? The three colors combine to make white light, revealing the image fully.

The Bible's genres and stories are like the different frequencies of light. On their own, they reveal some information, but not the whole picture or story. And it can be hard to see how some stories relate to the others at all. But that's like thinking green doesn't have any relationship with red or blue. If you want the whole picture, green must be in a relationship *with* red and blue.

Ultimately, the picture that's revealed in the stories of the Bible is the history of redemption, and redemption is only through Jesus. Each individual story and book is an episode in a much larger story. Sometimes it might be hard to see how the story reveals anything about Jesus, but Jesus is the ultimate embodiment of God's faithfulness to his people. And God's faithfulness is on display on every page of Scripture—even the book of Esther, which doesn't mention God's name at all.

John opens his Gospel by calling Jesus the Word by whom all things were made. At the Fall recorded in Genesis—the first book of the Bible—God promises that the seed of the woman will crush the serpent's head. Thousands of years later, Jesus fulfilled that promise on the cross. The people in between the promise and the cross looked forward to the Savior, although they couldn't see him clearly. The Old Testament is the story of God revealing more and more over time about the promised

Savior and the need for him. And during that time, God repeatedly proved he was faithful and trustworthy even when the promise of the Savior seemed dim. The New Testament is the continuation of that story after the promise is kept, spreading its good news to all people of the world until Jesus—as revealed in Revelation, the last book of the Bible—returns to reign forever.

As a result, the Bible isn't a random collection of unrelated stories like the Brothers Grimm. It's a collection of stories woven together by a single, larger story. And each individual story gets its meaning from the larger story, God's redemptive story.

WHY ARE THE OLD AND NEW TESTAMENTS SO DIFFERENT?

Imagine your great-great-grandchildren, what they'll look like and the world they'll live in. Now go even further and depict it somehow. Of course, every grandparent loves pictures of their grandchildren, but you can't take photographs of grandchildren that don't exist yet. So how will you depict them? Paint a picture? Write a song? Act out their life as a play? No matter how talented you are, none of these things will be anything other than symbols and shadows of what's to come. And when your great-great-grandchildren arrive, they will resemble how you pictured them in some ways, and surprise you in others.

Now imagine you're part of Israel in Old Testament times. You know there is a Messiah who will come, and you know quite a bit about what he'll be like. How would you depict him? The traditional understanding of the second commandment doesn't let you paint a picture of him, so that's out. Even if you were allowed to paint a picture, you'd get it wrong. But that doesn't matter because there are other kinds of pictures all around you, even though you may not fully realize what you're looking at.

Throughout Old Testament history, the Messiah is foreshadowed in many different ways using many different symbols. For example, the skin God gives Adam and Eve to cover themselves after they sin is symbolic of the blood atonement that would be central to the work of the Messiah. Prophets, priests, and kings each fulfilled some aspect of the Messiah. The ceremonies at the tabernacle and temple were temporary appeasements that pointed to the ultimate work of the Messiah.

In the New Testament, when the long-promised Messiah arrives, all the types, foreshadowing, and allusions suddenly come into sharp focus in the person of Jesus. It's like a backwards echo, where the Old Testament records the reflections of a sound that will happen in the future. Jesus is that sound. And because of his arrival, all the symbols that represented him and the work he would do (such as the temple ceremonies) are no longer necessary. The object of faith remains the same: the Messiah. But the way that faith in the Messiah is articulated and practiced changes. Abraham believed God, and it was credited to him as righteousness (Gal. 3:6). Who he had faith in is the same as New Testament believers, but how that faith is practiced is different.

Many aspects of the Old Testament are illuminated by the New Testament. And by reading the New Testament through the lens of the Old Testament, we can have a deeper understanding and appreciation of the fullness of God's revelation. Each lens on its own shows part of the picture but leaves the rest blurry. So even though the Old and New Testaments may appear different on a superficial level, they complement each other to create a complete picture.

ARE THE PROPHECIES IN THE BIBLE WORTH TAKING SERIOUSLY?

Sometimes we think of prophecy as a kind of fortune telling, but a prophecy is a message from God. This includes foretelling future events, but it also includes teaching and help for interpreting previous revelations. Because prophets spoke for God, to disobey or not believe a prophet was the same thing as disobeying or rejecting God. And in order to prove they had the authority to speak for him, God gave each prophet at least one sign or miracle to perform. Often, the sign was a prediction of a future event that would occur in the prophet's lifetime. If the event didn't come to pass or the prophet proclaimed even one thing falsely, they were to be put to death. So prophecies weren't made lightly.

The prophecies of future events have been a favorite target of skeptics. They often dismiss them as parts of the writings that were added in after the events already occurred, and that's why they were accurate. Or the language of the prophecy was so vague or used such symbolic language that it could apply to many different events. But history and archaeology have vindicated a number of prophecies that can't be so easily dismissed. Here are a couple of examples.

Ezekiel wrote a prophecy about the city of Tyre in chapter 26. Keep in mind that Tyre existed in two parts—a mainland section, and a section on a small island about a half-mile from shore. He said Tyre would be destroyed and attacked by many nations, that Nebuchadnezzar would attack it, that the stones from the city would be thrown in the water leaving Tyre a bare rock where fishing nets are spread, that it would never be rebuilt and no longer exist.

King Nebuchadnezzar attacked Tyre in 585 BC, destroying the city about eight years after the prophecy. Lucky guess? Keep reading. About 250 years later, Alexander the Great attacked the city. He threw the rubble left over from Nebuchadnezzar's attack into the water to make a causeway 200 feet wide that reached the island. Given that the water was only twenty feet deep, they had enough stones to do it. That cleared the former mainland city, making it a bare rock where fishermen spread nets even into the 20th century. The city was captured again in 314 BC and AD 1291. There is no way a later author could have added the prophecy to Scripture. Want to see the proof for yourself? Open Google Maps and search for "Tyre, Lebanon." You can see the causeway silted in to create an isthmus. The ancient city is still in ruins, with the modern city built around it.

Some of the most amazing prophecies were of the coming Messiah. There are at least 60 prophecies about what he would be like, when he would arrive, and what he would do. In the 1960s, mathematician Peter Stoner calculated the statistical probability of someone fulfilling just eight of them. The eight prophecies were (1) born in Bethlehem; (2) preceded by a messenger; (3) rode donkey into Jerusalem; (4) betrayed by a friend; (5) betrayed for 30 pieces of silver; (6) betrayer tries to return money, throwing silver coins on floor; (7) the Messiah would not speak to defend himself; 8) hands and feet would be pierced. After assigning conservative estimates for each prediction, and taking into account the population between when the prophecies were made and now, the odds are 1 in 10^{17} that they would be fulfilled by a single person. That's a 1 with 17 zeros. To conceive of that number, Stoner said to imagine a pile of silver dollars two feet deep all the way across the state of Texas, and one of the coins is painted red. Then imagine being blindfolded and allowed to pick just one coin from the pile. The odds of choosing the red coin is about 10^{17}. Imagine the odds of all 60 prophecies!

Not every fulfillment of prophecy has evidence like this, but these cases do show that prophecy can often be investigated. And if the evidence is compelling, then it should taken seriously.

DON'T THE GOSPELS CONTRADICT EACH OTHER?

Because the Bible is the primary authority for Christian doctrine and practice, we need to be able to trust that it's telling the truth. One of the tests for truth is noncontradiction. If a story contradicts itself, then something is wrong with it and we shouldn't trust it—especially if it's asking you to base your entire worldview on it. Often skeptics have accused the Gospels of being guilty of just that: contradicting each other.

Matthew and John claim to be eyewitnesses of the things they wrote about, while Mark and Luke are records of eyewitness accounts. The issue is that they record many of the same events, and sometimes the events differ in ways that are hard to reconcile. If they really were eyewitnesses, shouldn't their accounts match up?

A common example is the women who visited the tomb on Easter morning. Who was there and how many were there? At least four women are named, two are unnamed, and no two Gospels agree on the number or names except that they all include Mary Magdalene. Not only that, but Matthew mentions only one angel at the empty tomb, but John says there were two. If the Gospels can't even agree on the witness for the resurrection—the central event in Christianity—then how could they be trusted about anything else?

And there are many other issues like that. What time of day was Jesus crucified? Mark says it was the third hour, but John says Jesus was on trial at the sixth hour, which had to happen *before* the crucifixion. And what was written on the sign above Jesus while he hung on the cross? Each Gospel records something similar, yet different.

The answer to many of the apparent contradictions in the Gospels is that we're reading them through a lens of a modern view of history. We want to know *all* the facts, and we want to know them in order. We forget to appreciate that the Gospels were written by people who recorded history in different ways.

For example, they didn't think it was necessary to list every person present at an event. Sometimes, only the most important people to the writer of the story were mentioned. In the case of the women at the tomb, the Gospels all mention Mary Magdalene. And none of the Gospels claim their list includes the *only* women there. The same is true for the single angel mentioned by Matthew: he doesn't say there *wasn't* another angel present, which leaves the door open (so to speak) for John's second angel.

The sign above Jesus' head can be reconstructed by looking at all four citations at the same time. All say "the king of the Jews." They each contain additional words whose placement is obvious so that the entire message reads, "This is Jesus of Nazareth the king of the Jews." Clearly, each author abbreviated it while keeping the important, core message.

As for the time of crucifixion, Romans and Jews reckoned time in different ways. Roman days started at midnight, while Jewish days start at sunset or 6 pm. So when John says Jesus was on trial during the sixth hour, it would be 6 a.m. if the Roman method of time is used. And when Mark says the crucifixion happened at the third hour, it is the third hour of daylight, which is 9 a.m. in the Jewish reckoning of time. Both can be accurate without contradicting each other.

Although there are many other examples of apparent contradictions, they are just that: *apparent*—not actual—contradictions.

WHY SHOULD THE APOSTLES BE TRUSTED?

During his three years of ministry, Jesus taught many people, sometimes several thousand at a time. And a number of those probably heard him more than once. But there was a group of twelve men personally selected by Jesus to be specially trained by him. They traveled together, ministered together, learned together, and did life together.

Jesus gave this small group access to him in a way that no one else had. They received intense instruction and were able to ask him for clarification about his public teaching. They watched how he interacted with all kinds of people from different social stations, and they observed him in many different situations. Some of the most powerful miracles—such as walking on water or calming the storm—were witnessed only by them. They became better acquainted with Jesus' message and character than anyone else. In fact, after Jesus commanded the storm to calm, the twelve not only worshipped him as God, but Jesus accepted it—an acknowledgement of his deity.

At the discovery of the empty tomb, these were the people to whom the angels sent the women. And that evening, it was to this group of men that Jesus appeared. For forty days, he gave them many proofs that he was truly resurrected. But he mainly taught them truths they couldn't have understood before the resurrection. New teaching was revealed, and the instruction they received before his death took on new meaning.

At the end of the forty days, Jesus met them on a mountain and gave them final instructions. He commissioned them to spread his teaching throughout the world to make and baptize disciples. He gave them the authority to speak in his name, and he equipped them to do it. Then, before their eyes, he ascended into heaven. Ten days later, the Holy Spirit came and empowered them to act on that commission.

The Greek word for their special office is *apostle*, which means *messenger*. Given that Jesus is God incarnate, the second person of the Trinity, being sent by him is the same thing as being sent by God. In the Old Testament, a person given a message from God is a prophet. Therefore, the apostles are the New Testament equivalent of prophets. They had the authority to teach the message of Jesus, correct those who misunderstood it, and protect it from attack. No one else was equipped and commissioned for that work in such an authoritative way. True, Judas was not a true believer and fell away. But the remaining eleven, under the guidance of the Holy Spirit, replaced him with Matthias, a follower of Jesus from the beginning and witness of many of the same things.

In addition to these twelve, Jesus appeared to his brother, James, who became not only a believer, but an apostle. The only apostle to be commissioned after the forty days was Saul of Tarsus, who became known as Paul. The apostles radically reoriented their lives to focus on spreading the good news given to them by Jesus. And they were rewarded with hardship, torture, and eventually martyrdom, which indicates their conviction that what they were teaching was true. Although tradition varies about where the apostles travelled or how they were killed, only one—John—died of natural causes. All of them gave their lives for what they'd been taught and equipped for.

The earliest believers considered the teachings of these men as authoritative. They even collected their letters and writings. In some cases, the followers of the apostles—Mark and Luke—wrote down their teachings. These writings form the authority that the early church fathers appealed to as they explained and defended Christianity to a world that didn't know anything about it. The writings of the apostles were preserved and passed down, and are still the authority for the church today: the New Testament.

CHAPTER FOUR

Morality

ISN'T THE BIBLE'S VIEW OF SEXUALITY OVERLY RESTRICTIVE?

Have you ever tried to pound a nail with something other than a hammer? Have you ever used a magazine or newspaper to shield yourself from the rain? Maybe you've tried to open a locked window from the outside by sliding a driver's license between the sections. We've all taken things designed for a certain purpose and used them for something else. But what would you do if there was a disagreement about what something was originally designed for? The way to resolve it is to ask the designer what he intended.

As a part of creation, sexuality is a gift from God that can be used as he intended or abused—just like the rest of creation. So what did God say about sexuality? Everything we need to know is revealed in how God set up life in the Garden. God commanded Adam and Eve to be fruitful and multiply, and he equipped them to do it. At that time there was one man, one woman, and no other options. Two people of opposite sexes were all that was required to keep that commandment. And that design feature was reflected in the design of the living creatures they were stewards of. That design revealed sexuality has a utility, a work it is designed for, which is procreation. God also designed the work to be pleasurable. Although we were not made for the sole purpose of experiencing pleasure, it *is* part of our experience of how God designed the world, and therefore it's a good thing. But good things are only good in the context for which they were intended. A misused good thing becomes a bad thing. Truth can be used to mislead people, making it a lie. Medicine can be used to kill. And sexuality can be acted on in a way that wasn't intended.

In our culture, sexuality is not only acted on in a wide variety of ways, but celebrated. Anything goes. Except for the view that only one thing goes—God's way. The design of sexuality intended by God is at the core of the relationship that forms a family, the most basic unit in society. The misuse of sexuality undermines the stability of the family, and as a result, ultimately society itself.

When people act exclusively on pleasure, simply seeking what feels good, it has the appearance of freedom. But it keeps them from forming relationships that bring about a much greater good than their self-satisfaction. And it keeps them from contributing to the stability of society as a whole, which will limit them further. Acting on sexuality in ways other than God's plan *prevents* you from enjoying a number of very good things. In other words, it's overly restrictive. Biblical sexuality—God's plan—isn't restrictive at all. It's freedom from bad consequences.

ISN'T THE BIBLE'S VIEW OF GENDER OUTDATED AND OPPRESSIVE?

The Bible was written by heterosexual men and records the history of a male-dominated culture that often treated women as less valuable. To modern ears, it has homophobic language, and doesn't even touch on the possibility of someone being transgender. Today's culture is radically different. The heterosexual male-dominated world is an outdated notion, and homosexuality is now increasingly accepted and celebrated. And this new perspective acknowledges and embraces the fact that some boys identify more with girls, and vice versa. Some people are sexually attracted to both genders. So, skeptics ask, why let a book written 2,000–3,500 years ago by a group of homophobes dictate our view on gender?

It depends on what you mean by *gender*. Human beings have 23 pairs of chromosomes in their DNA that act as a biological blueprint. At conception, the twenty-third pair is formed by either two X chromosomes or an X and Y chromosome. There are no other combinations except in the case of a genetic disorder, which is—by definition—abnormal. A person with two X chromosomes is female, while a person with X and Y is male. These two sets are the variations within the category of gender—the biologically determined sex. A thousand years from now, if your DNA were to be examined, the lab scientist would be able to determine your gender. What they could never know from looking at your DNA is if you were attracted to people of the same gender, or if you identified with a different gender, or if you had gone through a sexual reassignment process that physically altered your body. The scientific advances of the last 50 years that allow for understanding DNA make the biblical understanding of gender anything but outdated, scientifically speaking.

Those who challenge the biblical view of sexuality use the word *gender* in a different way. Rather than being a useful category for distinguishing between the two biological variations of human beings, skeptics use gender to describe what they characterize as natural inclinations. They say they were born with the inclinations and therefore those inclinations are an intrinsic part of them. Some people claim to believe in God but also challenge the biblical view. They say if God made everything and is sovereign, then these inclinations can't be wrong, and therefore they reject the verses of the Bible that speak to that issue.

There are two problems with the non-biblical view. The first is scientific. Redefining *gender* doesn't change the fact that there are two and only two variations within human beings. It is—by definition—binary. It has nothing to do with natural inclinations or preferences, regardless of the word that's used. Appropriating words and redefining them doesn't escape the facts in play.

The second problem is a logical fallacy. Just because someone *is* a certain way doesn't mean they *ought* to be that way. When we say something ought to be a certain way, it means there's a law that governs our behavior before we act on it. It's a way to evaluate the choice to act or not. In other words, it's a moral law. And there cannot be a moral law without a law giver. You can't be the law giver, or your whims and preferences would be the law. It can't be society who makes moral law because majority rule is just a bigger version of the same problem. In fact, if society makes moral laws then no one has grounds to criticize the Bible's view of gender since Jewish society condemned alternate views of gender. It also erodes the justification of LGBTQ activism to impact and reform society. If the LGBTQ movement is in the minority, and the majority of society determines morality, then trying to reform it is—by definition—immoral.

Of course moral laws aren't like that. They aren't subject to individual whims or societal acceptance. They are laws that govern all people at all times in all places, can't change, and can't be other than what they are. In other words, they are transcendent and unchanging. They are also personal. So the source of morality must be personal, transcendent, and unchanging. In other words, morality must come from God. And his revelation about gender and sexuality is the standard by which we judge it.

The biblical view of non-biblical sexuality is the same as other non-biblical ideas: it's sin. But that's why the gospel is necessary. For ALL of us. There will be believers who struggle with gender and sexuality issues for their entire lives, just as we all have sins we will struggle against in ours. The Bible isn't oppressive, it's liberating. The gospel frees us from that bondage. Without the gospel, we freely choose the bondage and redefine it as freedom in order to live the lie.

DOESN'T THE BIBLE SUPPORT SLAVERY?

At its core, the offer of salvation is liberation from slavery to sin and its consequences. That's the symbolic meaning of the Exodus—the Jews coming out of slavery. That event is celebrated in the Passover, which is when Jesus was crucified to set all who would believe in him free from slavery. So the assumption is that slavery—to both sin and to earthly powers—is bad.

Yet, at the same time, the New Testament characterizes devotion and commitment to the faith as being a slave to the gospel. Not only is this metaphorical, drawing from a common cultural practice of the time, but the Greek word translated as *slave* can also be translated *servant*. Although there are important differences between slavery in the Roman Empire of the New Testament and the kind of slavery practiced in the British Empire and America, those distinctions don't exclude the abuse of human beings.

The problem skeptics have is with passages that address slavery. Slaves are owned by several heroes in the Old Testament. Despite having rights that protected them, and despite being freed after a certain number of years, slavery was a part of Israelite culture. In the New Testament, Jesus mentions slaves/servants in his parables. Paul mentions the issue several times in his letters, and one directly focuses on it. So isn't their lack of a clear condemnation of slavery a tacit approval of it?

When we read the Bible, we have to be able to discern the difference between prescription and description. Just because something is described in Scripture doesn't mean that's the way it should be. For example, Solomon (as well as others in the Old Testament) had many wives. Does that mean the Bible endorses polygamy? No. The whole of Scripture is clear on how marriage should look despite the abuses that are sometimes described.

The same can be said of slavery in Scripture. Just because it's acknowledged and described doesn't mean that slavery is morally acceptable. If the whole of biblical teaching is considered, it's clear that slavery is contrary to God's plan. Human beings were made in God's image. That's the one common denominator that defies time, place, and culture. That's why Paul (a purveyor of slavery, according to skeptics) wrote that we are one in Christ—no male or female, no Jew or Greek, and no slave or freeman. During the end times described in Revelation 18, when Babylon is judged, slave traders (part of the group of evil merchants aligned with Babylon) will weep and mourn.

More specifically, what exactly does Paul say to Philemon? Paul is writing from prison to the owner of a runaway slave. The slave, Onesimus, received the gospel from Paul and became a believer. And Paul is sending Onesimus back to his owner, Philemon, who himself is a Christian. Instead of overtly condemning slavery, Paul asks that Philemon receive Onesimus back as a brother in Christ. He doesn't deny his ownership in that system, but he does appeal for an uncommonly gracious treatment that—by example—actually undermines the system. If Paul were truly endorsing slavery, he wouldn't have appealed to Philemon on behalf of Onesimus. The appeal itself (which is the entirety of the book) is contrary to the status quo of the slavery of the day.

DOESN'T THE BIBLE'S VIEW OF SIN TEACH YOU TO HATE YOURSELF?

Another way to say *gospel* is *good news*. What makes good news good? It's given in a context of hardship, suffering, and uncertainty. In other words, to have good news you have to have bad news. Otherwise it's just plain news. In the Bible, what makes the good news of the gospel so good is the understanding of sin.

Because we were made in God's image, all people have an intuitive understanding of God's moral will. Different cultures or people might disagree about specific instances of right and wrong or the relevant facts, but everyone judges behavior in these categories whether or not they also think of it as God's moral will. God didn't merely design the physical world, he also designed how we should live and navigate it, including how we should treat him and other people. That's why to sin against someone else is also to sin against God.

Sometimes it means falling short or missing the mark, and sometimes it means intentionally ignoring our conscience, what we intuitively know to be right. You, me, and everyone we've ever met is a sinner. Except for Jesus, everyone who has ever lived—from the greatest moral hero to the worst serial killer—is a sinner. Because of the Fall of Adam in the garden, we inherited a sinful nature. That's why we sin.

Because he is perfectly good, righteous, and just, God hates sin and requires perfect obedience. We, too, should hate our sin. But since it's in our very nature, doesn't that mean we hate ourselves? Not at all.

When we sin, not only is it always against God, but it's also against ourselves. We were made to glorify God and enjoy him forever. Our sins keep us from doing that. We are most ourselves when we're obedient to God. The gifts we receive from him are the talents that bring us pleasure when we develop them, and bless the world around us. In a way, when we hate our sin, we hate who we're not. Our sins keep us from being who we were designed to be—conformed to the image of Christ.

The worst part of the problem of sin is that we cannot overcome it on our own. We don't have the ability because our natures are sinful. Left on our own, we can never truly be what we were designed to be. That is why we need a savior. We need rescuing from ourselves so we can truly be ourselves.

It's because we're made in his image that sinners are still loved by God and are so precious to him. How precious? He loved sinners so much he sent his own son, Jesus Christ, to take on the punishment for the sin of everyone who believes in him. Not only that, but his perfectly obedient, sinless life is credited to everyone who believes in him. And because of that, believers can stand before God fully themselves, unmarred by sin, reconciled to him in the perfect obedience of Christ. As a result, the best way to hate yourself is to *not* hate your sin.

DOESN'T THE BIBLE'S VIEW OF JUDGMENT TEACH YOU TO DESPISE NON-CHRISTIANS?

When Jesus was challenged by the scribes, Pharisees, and Sadducees, he called them snakes and asked how they would escape being condemned to hell. When he did miracles in towns that still rejected him, he passed judgment on them. When he prophesied the betrayal of Judas, he said it would be better if Judas had never been born. And he said anyone who rejects the Holy Spirit commits an unforgivable blasphemy. These are undeniably harsh words. If Christians are to be imitators of Christ, doesn't that mean we should hate unbelievers?

Not at all. With the exception of the judgment of Judas, most of the time when Jesus speaks like this, it was meant as a warning, not as a prophecy. We often speak the same way. Think about how many times as a kid you were doing something that made an adult say, "You'll shoot your eye out!" or "You'll break your neck!" They weren't foretelling the future as much as they were warning you of bad consequences if you didn't change your behavior. At times, Jesus used harsh words to confront hard hearts.

But harsh words weren't the only way Jesus confronted hard hearts. It wasn't even the main way. Remember, he's more than a good teacher and moral hero. Why was Jesus here in the first place? What was the point of his ministry? He is the Savior of the world, sent to die for the sins of all who would believe in him. And who needed saving? EVERYONE! His very presence was judgment not just on the people who witnessed his earthly ministry, but on every person who ever lived or will live on Earth. In other words, every Christian was once a non-Christian. And how did Jesus treat us? He loved us so much that he gave himself for us while we were still his enemies.

In light of that, Christians should do the same: love non-Christians. That's what Jesus did for us. And the best way to love them is to share the good news of the gospel with them. That can be done in many different ways, but the truth must always be spoken in love.

One of the most important things to keep in mind is that because human beings were made in the image of God, the knowledge of God is already known to them. The problem with unbelievers is not that they don't have enough knowledge about God. According to Romans 1:18 the problem is that they *do* have knowledge of God, but that they suppress it in unrighteousness. So when we share the gospel with unbelievers, we are revealing self-deceit, and that can be very painful to confront. Again, that's why the gospel must be spoken in love.

For Christians to despise non-Christians would be to ignore what Christ himself did for us and violate the Great Commission all believers have to spread the good news. The gospel can't be spread to people who already have it. And it can't be spread by those who despise those who need it. Judgment is real. That's the bad news. And that's what makes the gospel good news. And the good news is spread by people saved from judgment who proclaim the way of salvation to those who need it.

HOW CAN GOD BE LOVING WITH SO MUCH EVIL AND INJUSTICE IN THE WORLD?

How would you respond to this common argument? If God is all-powerful, then he has the ability to stop evil. And if God is also perfectly good, he would want to stop it. And yet evil and injustice still exist. Therefore God doesn't exist. Or, at best, he's not like the Bible says he is and therefore he's not worthy of worship.

Skeptics aren't the only people who wonder how evil and God can both exist. Many believers have struggled with this question when they were walking through periods of intense suffering. But not because the question can't be answered.

I once paid a woman thousands of dollars to cut open my toddler daughter with a knife and a saw. As you can imagine, my daughter suffered enormous pain. And the look in her eyes asked why I would let it happen. On the face of it, I sound like a moral monster. The woman I paid was, of course, a surgeon. And the procedure fixed a hole in my daughter's heart that not only threatened her life, but would have required additional open-heart surgeries to replace her valve every 10 or 15 years if this operation hadn't been done. The pain she experienced was far less than the pain she would suffer if she didn't undergo the procedure. I explained that to her, but as a thirteen-month-old, she didn't understand. All she knew was that she was in pain. She lacked the ability to understand the greater good being done. All she could do was trust me based on the love I had demonstrated to her throughout her life.

Sometimes when we experience evil and suffering we can't see the good that will result from it. We don't see God at work. But that doesn't mean he *isn't* working and there is *no* good. To say there is no good that comes from our suffering, or that there is no justification for it is an argument from ignorance. Being transcendent and all-knowing gives God a great advantage on the whole context we don't have.

But we do have experience with God, and that tells us he is engaged, good, loving, forgiving, and powerful. He has also revealed himself that way in Scripture, adding more information such as his omnipotence, omniscience, perfect righteousness, and sovereignty. Because he's sovereign, the evil we see and experience cannot be outside his control. So for God to really be who Scripture says he is, there must be a reason for evil, and its existence must bring about a greater good. The evil is justified. That's the truth we cling to when we aren't allowed the see the good in the suffering we experience.

The best example is found in the greatest evil ever committed: the crucifixion of Jesus. He wasn't merely innocent of the crimes of sedition and blasphemy; he was perfect. He never sinned. Yet God incarnate was brutally tortured, then executed in a manner designed to inflict maximum pain for a long period. If you had been at the cross, you would have witnessed the greatest evil ever committed, but also the greatest good ever accomplished. But you wouldn't have realized it. The context and meaning were made clear three days later, and even then it had to be explained and wrestled with.

Here's another glimpse behind the curtain. Some of the most important attributes of God couldn't be known without evil. For example, God is forgiving, merciful, and gracious. We couldn't know God's forgiveness without doing something to be forgiven for. We couldn't receive mercy unless we deserved punishment, and grace wouldn't be gracious if we deserved his favor. Although God had nothing to forgive before the Fall, his offering forgiveness doesn't mean he changed in his essential being to offer it. This is because forgiveness is an expression of love, a variety of it. Love is an essential characteristic of God that never changes. God loved us so much that while we were his enemies, he pursued us. That's why we love him—because he loved us first. Does that justify our sin since more sin reveals more forgiveness? Of course not. But we learn things about God's character and how much he loves us through our sin that we wouldn't otherwise know.

For the skeptic, this question is extremely difficult. What do they mean by *evil*? And is injustice bad? For the skeptic's question to make sense, they have to define *evil* and *bad*. The problem is that they can't. Good and evil are moral concepts that require a transcendent, perfect, personal being as their source. Good and evil can't be mere personal preference or the majority rules of society. Those things change or could be something other than what they are. But good and evil aren't those kinds of things. For example, there's never a time or context where injustice is morally good. And there's never a time or context where evil (such as murder or rape) is morally good. Without God to ground those moral laws and concepts, they are meaningless. Ironically, evil is one of the best pieces of evidence *for* God, not against him.

Although the problem of evil can be answered, it's often the wrong answer to give if you're trying to comfort someone who is suffering. Their problem isn't logical or philosophical, it's existential and experiential. Sometimes people see evil and ask, *Where is God?* The answer is on the cross. Jesus died not only for the sins of all who would believe in him, but he's making all things right. He suffered on the cross for every natural evil. The world will be restored through the work of Christ on the cross. Where is God? Suffering right along with you, calling you closer to him through it.

Made in the USA
Middletown, DE
31 January 2022